MW00770612

TO

Desiree Pittman

FROM

Leip Gogaloa

DATE

June 21, 2024

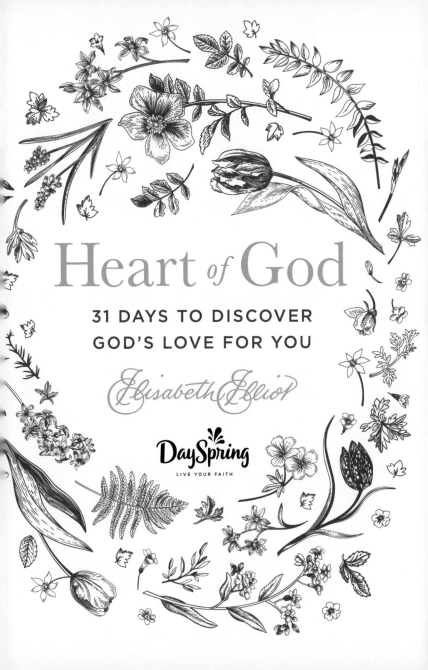

Heart *of* God

31 DAYS TO DISCOVER
GOD'S LOVE FOR YOU

Elisabeth Elliot

DaySpring

LIVE YOUR FAITH

Heart of God: 31 Days to Discover God's Love for You
Copyright © 2022 The Elisabeth Elliot Foundation.
All rights reserved.
First Edition, September 2022

Published by

21154 Highway 16 East
Siloam Springs, AR 72761
dayspring.com

Written by: Elisabeth Elliot
Cover Design by: Gayle Raymer

Printed in China
Prime: J9336
ISBN: 978-1-64870-847-3

Contents

Foreword

This precious thirty-one day devotional was unearthed completely by accident, yet all within God's divine providence. Back to the Bible (producers of the radio program Gateway to Joy with Elisabeth Elliot from 1988 to 2001) found this piece tucked away on a Word document that Elisabeth had created at some point when she was broadcasting GTJ. It was brought to the attention of the Elisabeth Elliot Foundation, and we realized that the writing had never before been published or seen. What a treasure not only to have an unpublished work but that it was written in a format much like the devotionals being published today by contemporary Christian authors. Our Elisabeth was ahead of her time.

May you be encouraged, as we were, by these fresh yet timeless truths Elisabeth and others share…to draw us ever close to the heart of God.

Grace & Peace,

THE ELISABETH ELLIOT FOUNDATION

In the movie *The Passion of the Christ*, the crucifixion scene is brought to a close by a large teardrop that splashes down from heaven. The teardrop is a prelude to a violent storm and earthquake that drive all but Jesus' most committed disciples from the foot of the cross. While fictional, the teardrop is a dramatic reminder that God has a heart—a heart broken by man's sin.

As we study the Bible, we find a multitude of references, either directly or indirectly, that reveal God's heart. This book examines the heart of God through thirty-one devotional readings. Each brief chapter contains Bible verses, a short essay, quotations from noted Christian thinkers, and a prayer. Each chapter is a powerful reminder that God's heart reflects His character. If we want to know God better, we need to know His heart.

Your heavenly Father loves you in ways that you cannot fully understand. God's heart is filled with care, concern, compassion, empathy, and love. As you read these pages, carefully consider what God's love means to you. And remember: if you genuinely trust your heavenly Father, and if you allow His Son to reign over your life, you will be held close to God's heart—today, tomorrow, and forever.

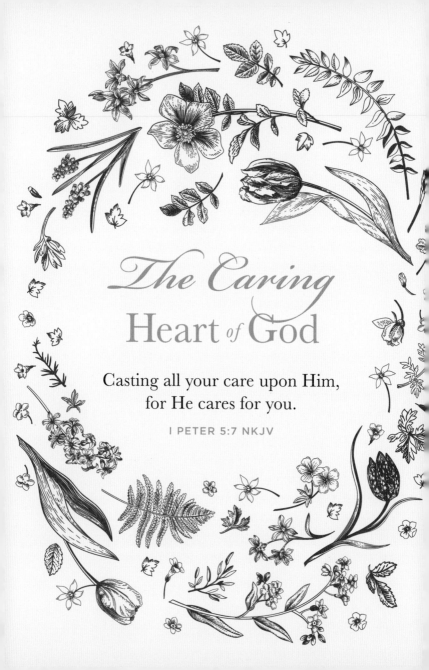

The Caring
Heart of God

Casting all your care upon Him,
for He cares for you.

I PETER 5:7 NKJV

Do you ever have those days when you wonder if anyone cares for you? You can be certain that the heart of God cares for you. God's heart is tender and loving. God cares for us when no one else seems to be concerned. When you and I offer our fears, worries, and anxieties to God, we give Him the opportunity to demonstrate how marvelously caring His heart really is, and we allow God to show us how deeply He cares for us.

Peter tells us to "cast" all our cares. This word carries with it the idea of deliberately depositing a burden upon someone or something else. If we were to do that to another person, that person might feel like we were imposing. But it is not so with God. Peter tells us to actually cast it or throw it upon God, who will never feel imposed upon because He cares for us.

Have you humbly opened your heart to Him? Have you taken your worries to Him? Have you accepted the outpouring of loving care that flows from God's heart? If not, then today is the perfect time to do so. Cast your cares upon God and leave them there. When you do, you will experience relief like a heavy load has been lifted from your shoulders. And it has, because the heart of God cares for you.

If you wish to leave *much wealth* to your children, leave them in *God's care*.

JOHN CHRYSOSTOM

A life spent in the service of God and communion with Him is the most pleasant life that anyone can live in this world.

MATTHEW HENRY

Cast your cares on God; **that anchor holds.**

ALFRED, LORD TENNYSON

Praise the Father for His loving kindness; tenderly cares He for His erring children. Praise Him.

ELIZABETH R. CHARLES

The work of the Spirit of God is not only to save souls but also to care and cultivate the face of the earth, the material world.

TIMOTHY KELLER

God, Your loving care for me is deeper than I can imagine. Thank You for caring about me when no one else seems to. I will open my heart to You, and I will return Your love today, tomorrow, and throughout eternity. Amen.

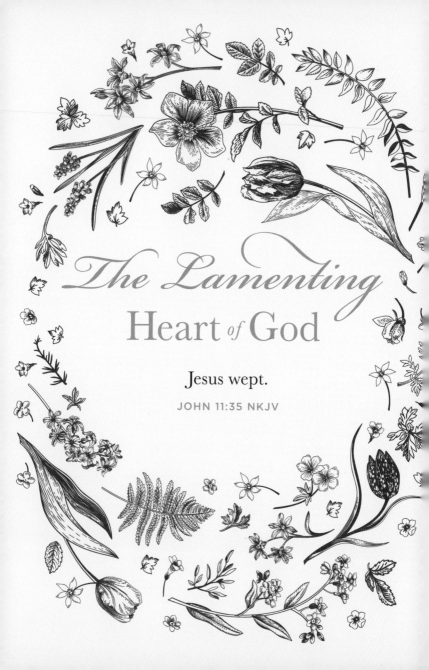

The Lamenting Heart of God

Jesus wept.

JOHN 11:35 NKJV

When Christ stood outside the tomb of Lazarus, the brother of Martha and Mary, He was overcome with grief, and He wept. Even though Jesus knew that He was going to raise His friend from the dead, the realization of how sin had caused such misery and suffering, ending in death, ripped His heart apart.

Jesus' response to the death of Lazarus gives us insight into the heart of God: God's heart is a lamenting heart. It feels our pain. When we experience the pangs of human suffering, God suffers with us. When we grieve at the loss of our loved ones, God understands our sadness. He feels it as well, and He stands ready to comfort us whenever we sincerely turn to Him.

Are you sorrowing today? Know that God feels that sorrow too. Give that grief to the One who knows your pain. Then, in His own perfect time and in His own perfect way, He will heal your pain *if* you invite Him to rule over your heart, life, and soul.

Our loving Lord is not just present, but
nearer than the thought can imagine—
so near that a whisper can reach Him.

AMY CARMICHAEL

Let my heart be broken by the things
that break the *heart of God*.

BOB PIERCE

There is a joy available that the deepest
grief cannot put out. No circumstance or
person can take away the joy God gives.

TIMOTHY KELLER

When you have *nothing left* but God,
then you become aware that
God is enough.

MAUDE ROYDEN

God is not a power or principle or law, but
He is a living, creating, communicating
person—a mind who thinks, a heart who feels,
a will who acts, whose best name is Father.

ROBERT HAMILL

*Lord, it is sometimes more than I can comprehend that
You would be willing to connect Your heart to mine in
such a way that You feel all that I feel. Your willingness
to share in my sorrow and grief makes me love You even
more. May I praise Your holy name forever. Amen.*

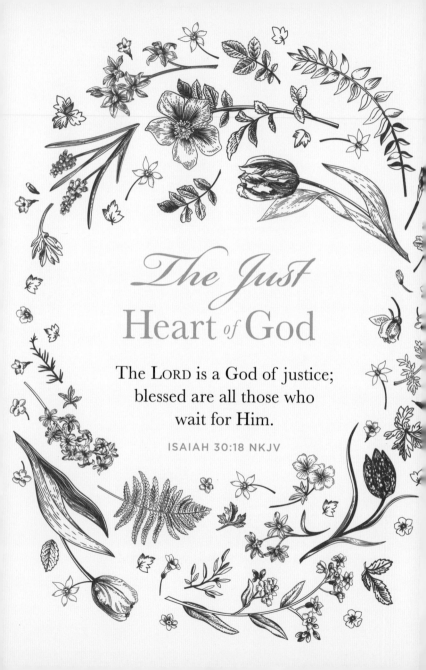

The Just Heart of God

The LORD is a God of justice;
blessed are all those who
wait for Him.

ISAIAH 30:18 NKJV

Have you ever been in a position where something unjust happened to you? Have you ever been unjustly criticized or wrongly accused? And then, have you wondered what you should do about it? Sometimes the best thing you can do is turn matters over to God. Why? Because the heart of God is just—and God always makes things right in due time.

There has never been a time when God was not a just God. Moses said it this way to the people of Israel: "Ascribe greatness to our God. He is the Rock, His work is perfect; for all His ways are justice, a God of truth and without injustice; righteous and upright is He" (Deuteronomy 32:3–4 NKJV).

Moses was convinced that God was a God of justice, and we, too, must be convinced of that fact, even though we might not always see that justice at work. Sometimes you get cheated. Sometimes things happen in your life that you can't understand. Sometimes you say, "God, don't You see what they're doing to me?" Sometimes you're just baffled, and you become impatient waiting for God to act. If so, be patient. Remember that God's timing is not our timing.

If we had our way, we would balance the books of justice much sooner than He does. Truthfully, we should probably be more cautious in our calls for God's justice. None of us would fare very well if He were to immediately enforce justice for every act of sin or evil.

Make no mistake about it, though. God's heart is set on justice. The books will balance. We can depend on Him to set all things in order.

To serve God is nothing else than to maintain and *preserve justice* by good works.

LACTANTIUS

God, our loving, caring, faithful, holy, and just God, has shaped a plan that will lead to victory, hope, peace, and joy. All of it takes shape under His mighty hand, as we surrender our wills to His.

CHARLES SWINDOLL

God's compassion flows out of His goodness,
and goodness without justice is not goodness.
God spares us because He is good, but He
could not be good if He were not just.

A. W. TOZER

Man is unjust, but *God is just*;
and finally justice triumphs.

HENRY WADSWORTH LONGFELLOW

Dear Father of justice, help me to wait patiently for Your plans to unfold. And when there is injustice in this world, when there are people who are oppressed and in need, use me as an agent of change. May Your justice reign in my life and Your world, now and forever. Amen.

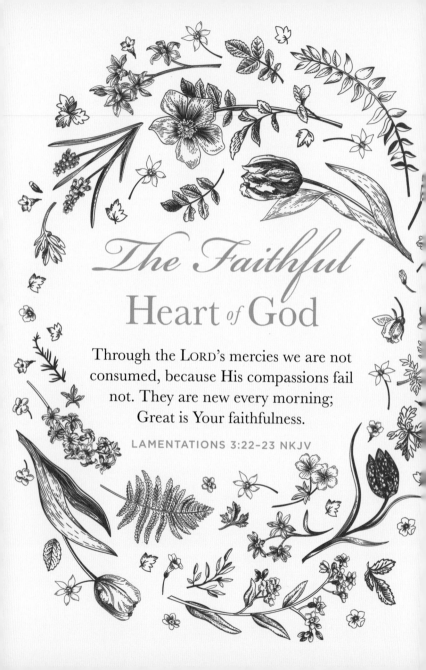

The Faithful
Heart of God

Through the LORD's mercies we are not
consumed, because His compassions fail
not. They are new every morning;
Great is Your faithfulness.

LAMENTATIONS 3:22–23 NKJV

The Bible makes it perfectly clear that the heart of God is always faithful. The faithfulness of God does not mean we, His children, are freed from life's problems and tragedies. It means that God will preserve us *in* our difficulties, not *from* our difficulties.

God's faithfulness is made clear in the beautiful words of Psalm 23:4: "Yea, though I walk through the valley of the shadow of death, I will fear no evil: for Thou art with me; Thy rod and Thy staff they comfort me" (KJV). God does not exempt us from the valleys of life, but neither does He ask us to walk alone. He is always there.

God's heart is faithful to His people, He is faithful to His Word, and He is faithful to you. Paul writes in I Corinthians 1:9, "God is faithful, by whom you were called into the fellowship of His Son, Jesus Christ our Lord" (NKJV). God has a faithful heart. Trust Him, and take comfort in the unerring promises and the never-ending faithfulness of your Lord.

People . . . think they are apart from God—
so far apart that they cannot follow Him.
Let no one think that! . . . Consider that God
is near you, for great harm comes of feeling that
God is distant. For let a man go away or
come back: God never leaves.

MEISTER ECKHART

Tell of His wondrous *faithfulness*
And sound His pow'r abroad;

Sing the sweet promise of His grace,
The *love and truth* of God.

ISAAC WATTS

God's faithfulness has never depended on the
faithfulness of His children. . . . God is greater
than our weakness. In fact, I think it is our
weakness that reveals how great God is.

MAX LUCADO

In *God's faithfulness*
lies eternal security.

CORRIE TEN BOOM

Your faithfulness, Lord, is everlasting. You are faithful
to me even when I am not faithful to You. Today, let
me serve You faithfully with my heart, my soul, and
my mind. And then, let me rest in the knowledge of
Your unchanging and faithful love for me. Amen.

The Shepherding
Heart *of* God

I am the good shepherd. The good
shepherd gives His life for the sheep.

JOHN 10:11 NKJV

The heart of God is a shepherd's heart. Shepherds were known for the sacrificial care they gave to their flocks. No matter how unpleasant the weather, the shepherd was there to care for his sheep. If a sheep became lost, the shepherd left those who were safe and went out to find the one in trouble. When fresh pasture or clean water was needed, it was the shepherd who led the way. When danger appeared on the horizon, it was this servant of the sheep who stood between his flock and whatever threatened the animals under his care. Sometimes that meant even putting his own life on the line. But that's what a good shepherd did.

Our heavenly Father is the supreme Good Shepherd who always cares for His flock. Others might serve as His undershepherds and, as such, should be respected. But the ultimate care of the flock rests with the shepherd heart of our God.

Do you have a need? Then look to your Shepherd. Are you feeling threatened or insecure? Then look to the Caretaker of the flock. Whatever the circumstances, you can trust the One who has a shepherd's heart. He has already laid down His life for you. How much more will He provide and care for your needs?

Jesus is the only shepherd who knows what it is like to be a sheep (John 10:11). He understands what we are going through and will be with us every step of the way, even through death itself.

TIMOTHY KELLER

It was not the soldiers who killed Him, nor the screams of the mob; it was *His devotion to us*.

MAX LUCADO

Back when the sacred authors used the imagery of the shepherd to depict Jesus, they had a clear understanding of the job description. A shepherd is needed only when there are no fences. He is someone who stays with his sheep at all cost, guiding, protecting, and walking with them through the fields. He's not just a person who raises sheep.

LENA WOLTER

At the heart of the gospel is a God who deliberately surrenders to the wild, irresistible *power of love*.

PHILIP YANCEY

The Lord my pasture shall prepare,
and feed me with a shepherd's care;
His presence shall my wants supply,
and guard me with a watchful eye.

JOSEPH ADDISON

Dear God, You are not only the Good Shepherd—You are my Good Shepherd. Help me to trust You with all my needs and learn to follow You wherever You lead. When danger threatens, may I run to You and find safety and protection. Amen.

Our heavenly Father
wants nothing but the best
for any of us, and only He
knows what that is, for He is
All-wise, *the Omniscient*.

ELISABETH ELLIOT

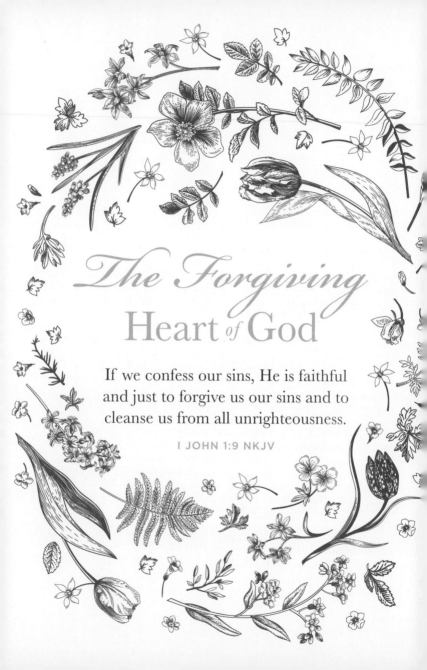

The Forgiving
Heart of God

If we confess our sins, He is faithful
and just to forgive us our sins and to
cleanse us from all unrighteousness.

I JOHN 1:9 NKJV

The heart of God is a forgiving heart. He loves to forgive. We may have just made the biggest mistake of our life, but God will forgive us if we repent. Sin grieves God's heart, but God loves to forgive even in the midst of His grief.

The word *forgive* means "to release." To forgive is to let go of a debt. It means to not demand payment of a debt. Somebody hurts you, and instead of retaliating, you say to God, "I give this hurt to You. I release it. It's off my shoulders. God, You do with it whatever You want." Real forgiveness is when you say, "It's no longer my business; it's God's. I'm not going to collect on the debt."

In Luke 23 Jesus hangs on the cross. Crucified with Him are two criminals, one on His right and one on His left. Jesus is dying with thieves, men who are the outcasts of society. He's hanging on a cross between two men who belong there—but He doesn't! And amazingly, Jesus says, "Father, forgive them, for they do not know what they do" (Luke 23:34 NKJV). I have always been amazed by that verse. Jesus was hanging on the cross absolutely and totally innocent, asking the Father to forgive people who were not innocent. When people were at their worst, Jesus was at His best saying, "Father, forgive them."

If you've been to Calvary and received the forgiveness of God, then adopt the heart of God; since you've been forgiven, it's time to become a forgiver. And remember: there's nothing more tender than the forgiving heart of God.

The eternal plan to reconcile man with God and bridge the separation, to save him from judgment for that sin, to forgive him of all sins, originated in the heart of God.

ANNE GRAHAM LOTZ

Jesus was put through awful, awful torture, and He did that for me, and He chose to forgive me. And if He chose to forgive me for all I've done, then certainly I can turn around and forgive others. And that's where that grace flows from Him through me to others.

RUTH BELL GRAHAM

God is glorified when people believe His gospel, love His Son, and accept His diagnosis of their greatest need, which is *forgiveness of sin*.

JOHN MACARTHUR

We do not have to make God willing to forgive. In fact, it is God who is working to make us willing to seek His forgiveness.

RICHARD FOSTER

Where is the *foolish person* who would think it in his power to commit a sin more than *God could forgive*?

ST. FRANCIS DE SALES

Heavenly Father, forgiveness is Your commandment, and I know that I need to forgive others just as You have forgiven me. But genuine, lasting forgiveness is difficult. Help me to forgive those who have injured me, and deliver me from the traps of anger and bitterness. Sometimes, I feel the strong desire to strike out against those who have hurt me, but You command me to turn away from revenge. Help me remember, Lord, that I am never fully liberated until I have been freed from the prison of hatred—and that You offer me that freedom through Your Son, Jesus Christ. Amen.

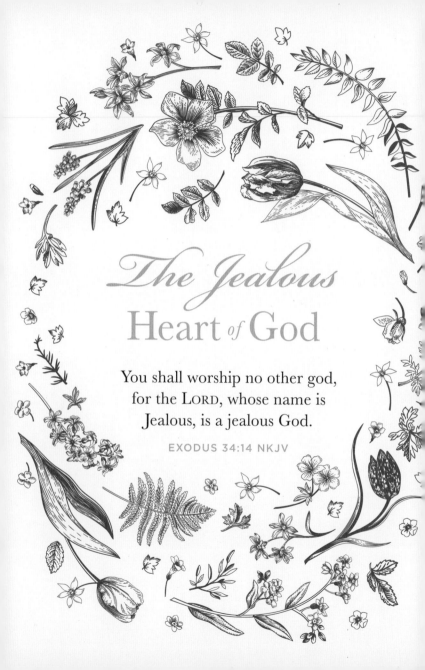

The Jealous
Heart of God

You shall worship no other god,
for the LORD, whose name is
Jealous, is a jealous God.

EXODUS 34:14 NKJV

Our loving heavenly Father is a compassionate God who seeks the very best for us. Because of this, however, our Creator is also a jealous God who intends that we worship Him and only Him. God's jealousy, however, should not be interpreted as a sign that God is uncaring or sinister. God's jealousy is a righteous jealousy for His people. God wants what is best for us, and what is best is this: nothing other than God.

It makes the heart of God jealous when we make gods out of anything but Him. It makes the heart of God jealous when our possessions possess us. God is jealous for our attention, for our love, and for our worship. Because He is some kind of egomaniac? No! On the contrary, He wants us to receive the very best—*Him*!

May we, as believers who have been saved by the blood of a risen Christ, recognize that what God has to offer is the very best. And may we never make Him jealous by running after worthless things instead of Him.

God knows that the best possible thing *for us* is to be absolutely taken up and obsessed with Him. He knows that He's the ultimate source of all our joy and comfort, and wants us to come to the source.

MIKE TAYLOR

Even God attributes to Himself avarice, jealousy, anger; and *these are virtues* as well as kindness, pity, constancy.

BLAISE PASCAL

[God's] jealousy does not grow out of insecurity, anxiety, frustration, covetousness, pride, or spite, as ours usually does. It is the natural and necessary by-product of His absolute sovereignty and infinite holiness.

RICHARD L. STRAUSS

**For the *Lord your God* is
a consuming fire, *a jealous God*.**

DEUTERONOMY 4:24 NKJV

If God is jealous herein, we should be so, afraid
of offering any worship to God otherwise
than as He has appointed in His Word.

MATTHEW HENRY

*Dear Lord, You are right in Your jealousy. I will have
no other gods before You. Jesus paid the greatest price
when He died on a cross for my sins. He endured
indignity, suffering, and death so that I might live.
Therefore, I will focus my devotion and love on You
alone. You deserve all my attention, allegiance, and
affection. My heart and life are Yours forever. Amen.*

The Humble
Heart of God

Let this mind be in you which was also in Christ Jesus, who, being in the form of God, did not consider it robbery to be equal with God, but made Himself of no reputation, taking the form of a bondservant, and coming in the likeness of men. . . . He humbled Himself and became obedient to the point of death, even the death of the cross.

PHILIPPIANS 2:5–8 NKJV

It's not unusual for God's sovereignty to be born through humility. Consider God's sovereignty and the humility that is found in the person of Jesus Christ. They almost contradict each other. In Jesus we have the sovereign God—who humbles Himself. The *sovereign* God has a *humble* heart. What a remarkable truth!

Philippians 2:5–8 details the humble heart of God. Each phrase is significant. The passage starts with "Let this mind be in you which was also in Christ Jesus, who, being in the form of God" (NKJV). The word that is translated as "form" speaks of a change in form. Some translations use the word nature here. But the verse is not talking about God's nature; it's talking about the form in which we perceive God's nature. Nature describes essence; form describes how we view that essence. The word here clearly means the form of God, not the nature of God. To be sure, Jesus is by nature God. But this phrase speaks of Jesus being in the form of God and then changing.

John tells us that "God is Spirit" (John 4:24 NKJV). Apparently, we are to understand that before Jesus became a man, He was Spirit. The writer of Philippians goes on: Jesus, "being in the form of God, did not consider it robbery to be equal with God." Other versions of the Bible translate this as "did not consider equality with God something to be grasped" (NIV). I think "grasped" is a better translation here. The word means to lay your hands on something, to cling to. Jesus, in the form of God, did not think that form was something He had to tenaciously cling to in order to be God. In other words, He could give up the free form of a spirit and still be God; He could take a body of flesh and remain equally God. He didn't need to cling to the form of God in order to retain what it means to be God.

So, Christ gave up that form and "made Himself of no reputation." He "made Himself nothing" (NIV). The idea here is that of "emptying." Jesus emptied Himself and came to earth to live among us and die for us. The Giver of Life, the One who created life, the sovereign God submitted Himself to obedience and death, but not just any old death—not a quiet death during His sleep or a wayward donkey accident. He submitted Himself to death, "even the death of the cross," the most cruel, violent, wicked, abominable death known to mankind.

Marvel at the humble heart of God!

Jesus had a *humble heart*. **If He abides in us, pride will never dominate our lives.**

BILLY GRAHAM

We see how Jesus clearly chooses the way of humility. He does not appear with great fanfare as a powerful savior, announcing a new order. On the contrary, he comes quietly, with the many sinners who are receiving a baptism of repentance.

HENRI NOUWEN

Humility is the exhibition of the spirit of Jesus Christ and is the touchstone of saintliness.

OSWALD CHAMBERS

Heavenly Father, Jesus clothed Himself with humility when He chose to come to this earth so that He might live and die for all creation. Christ is my Master and my example. Clothe me with humility, Lord, so that I might be more like Your Son. Amen.

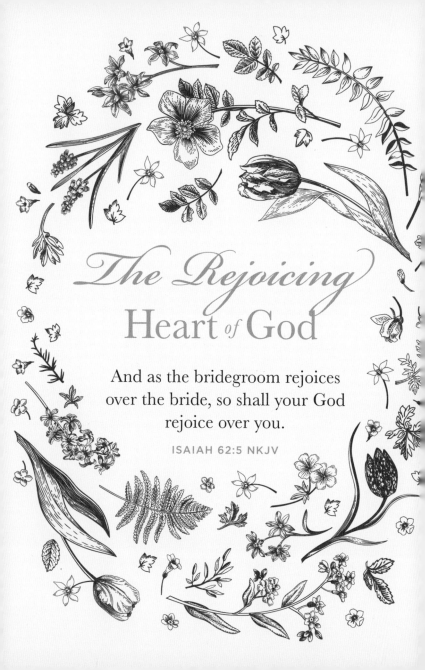

The Rejoicing
Heart *of* God

And as the bridegroom rejoices
over the bride, so shall your God
rejoice over you.

ISAIAH 62:5 NKJV

My grandfather was a Baptist deacon. He was a simple man, an electrician by trade. And he used to say something that I haven't heard in a long time: "No Bible, no breakfast!" Those words are still right on target. When we, like my grandfather, place our love for God above our own personal desires, God rejoices!

When the Lord is in the midst of a people who worship Him in a spirit of humility and love, His heart overflows with joy. The psalmist says it this way:

> The LORD your God in your midst,
> The Mighty One, will save;
> He will rejoice over you with gladness,
> He will quiet you with His love,
> He will rejoice over you with singing.
> *Zephaniah 3:17* NKJV

Do you sincerely want God to rejoice over you? Then live righteously. Allow God to preside over every aspect of your life. And what you'll find is that it's a two-way street. As you give God reason to rejoice over you, you will find your own heart filled with joy.

Why not get started today? Ask God to show you some specific ways you can cause His heart to rejoice today.

Joy can be the echo of
God's life within you.

DUANE PEDERSON

The LORD will again rejoice over you for good as He rejoiced over your fathers, if you obey the voice of the LORD your God, to keep His commandments and His statutes which are written in this Book of the Law, and if you turn to the LORD your God with all your heart and with all your soul.

DEUTERONOMY 30:9-10 NKJV

Joy is not gush. **Joy is not mere jolliness. Joy is perfect acquiescence—acceptance, rest—in** *God's will,* **whatever comes.**

AMY CARMICHAEL

Christ and joy **go together.**

E. STANLEY JONES

All movements of discipleship arrive at a place where joy is experienced. Every step of assent toward God develops the capacity to enjoy. Not only is there, increasingly, more to be enjoyed, there is steadily the acquired ability to enjoy it.

EUGENE PETERSON

Dear Lord, it is my heart's desire to live in such a way that You can rejoice over me. May You develop in me through Your Holy Spirit those things that would bring joy to Your heart. And as You rejoice, may I also feel the joy of Your pleasure. May I rejoice with You and give You the praise and the glory forever. Amen.

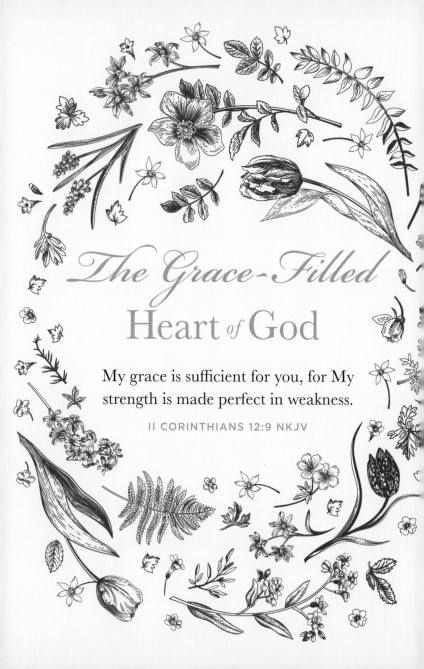

The Grace-Filled
Heart *of* God

My grace is sufficient for you, for My
strength is made perfect in weakness.

II CORINTHIANS 12:9 NKJV

The grace of God overflows from His heart. And if we open our hearts to Him, we receive His grace, and we are blessed with joy, abundance, peace, and eternal life.

The familiar words of Ephesians 2:8 make God's promise perfectly clear: "For by grace you have been saved through faith, and that not of yourselves; it is the gift of God" (NKJV). In other words, we are saved, not by our actions, but by God's mercy. We are saved, not because of our good deeds, but because of our faith in Christ.

God's grace is the ultimate gift, a gift beyond comprehension and beyond compare. And because it is the ultimate gift, we owe God the ultimate in thanksgiving.

God's grace is indeed a gift from the heart—*God's heart*. And as believers, we must accept God's precious gift thankfully, humbly, and immediately—today is never too soon because tomorrow may be too late.

The grace of God runs downhill toward the ones who are emptied and vulnerable, toward the ones who admit that they struggle.

ANGELA THOMAS

Thank God, He doesn't **measure out grace in teaspoons.**

AMY CARMICHAEL

God's grace and power seem to reach their peak when we are at our weakest point.

ANNE GRAHAM LOTZ

Grace grows best in the winter.

C. H. SPURGEON

There is *no evil* that the Father's love cannot pardon and cover, there is *no sin* that is a match for *His grace*.

TIMOTHY KELLER

Accepting Your grace can be hard, Lord. Somehow, I feel that I must earn Your love and Your acceptance. Yet, the Bible makes this glorious promise: You love me and save me by Your grace. It is a gift I can only accept and not earn. Thank You, dear Lord, for Your gift of grace. Amen.

I believe that in every
time and place it is within our
power to acquiesce in the will
of God—and *what peace
it brings* to do so!

ELISABETH ELLIOT

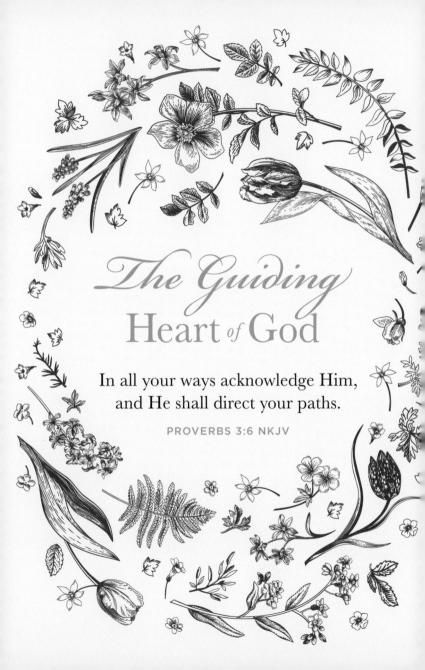

The Guiding
Heart of God

In all your ways acknowledge Him,
and He shall direct your paths.

PROVERBS 3:6 NKJV

When we genuinely seek to know the heart of God—when we prayerfully seek His wisdom and His will—our heavenly Father carefully guides us over the peaks and valleys of life. Whether we find ourselves at the pinnacle of the mountain or the darkest depths of the valley, the guiding heart of God is always there to rejoice with us or comfort us.

As Christians whose salvation has been purchased by the blood of Christ, we have every reason to live joyously and courageously. After all, Christ has already fought and won our battle for us—He did so on the cross at Calvary. But despite Christ's sacrifice, and despite God's promises, we may become confused or disoriented by the endless complications and countless distractions of life here in the twenty-first century.

If you're unsure of your next step, lean upon God's promises and lift your prayers to Him. Remember that God is always near; remember that He is your Protector and your Deliverer. Open yourself to His heart, and trust Him to guide your path. When you do, the guiding heart of God will direct your steps, and you will receive His blessings today, tomorrow, and throughout eternity.

God will prove to you how good and acceptable and perfect His will is when He's got His hands on the steering wheel of your life.

STUART AND JILL BRISCOE

Make my path sure, O Lord. Establish my goings. Send me when and where You will, and manifest to all that *Thou are my guide*.

JIM ELLIOT

It's a bit like river rafting with an experienced guide. You may begin to panic when the guide steers you straight into a steep waterfall, especially if another course appears much safer. Yet, after you've emerged from the swirling depths and wiped the spray from your eyes, you see that just beyond the seemingly "safe" route was a series of jagged rocks. Your guide knew what he was doing after all.

SHIRLEY DOBSON

The Bible is not a guidebook to a theological museum. It is a road map showing us the way into neglected or even forgotten glories of the living God.

RAYMOND ORTLUND

Men give advice; *God gives guidance.*

LEONARD RAVENHILL

Lord, You have a plan for my life that is grander than I can imagine. Let Your purposes be my purposes. Let Your will be my will. When I am confused, give me clarity. When I am frightened, give me courage. Let me be Your faithful servant, always seeking Your guidance for my life. And let me always be a shining beacon for Your Son, Christ Jesus, today and every day that I live. Amen.

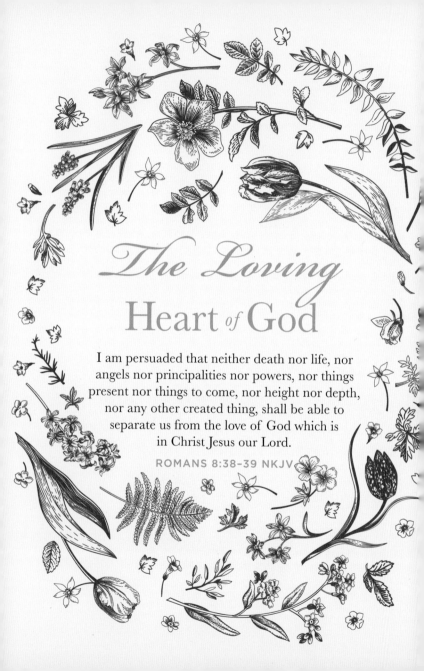

The Loving
Heart of God

I am persuaded that neither death nor life, nor
angels nor principalities nor powers, nor things
present nor things to come, nor height nor depth,
nor any other created thing, shall be able to
separate us from the love of God which is
in Christ Jesus our Lord.

ROMANS 8:38–39 NKJV

The words of I John 4:8 teach us that "he who does not love does not know God, for God is love" (NKJV). And because we can be assured that God is love, we can also be assured that God's heart is a loving heart.

God loves you. He loves you more than you can imagine; His affection is deeper than you can fathom. God made you in His own image and gave you salvation through the person of His Son Jesus Christ. And as a result, you have an important decision to make. You must decide what to do about God's love: Will you return it . . . or not?

When you accept the love that flows from the heart of God, you are transformed. When you embrace God's love, you feel differently about yourself, your neighbors, your community, your church, and your world. When you open your heart to God's love, you feel compelled to share God's message—and His compassion—with others.

God's heart is overflowing with love . . . for *you*! Accept that love. Return that love. And share that love. Today.

O Love that will not let me go,
I rest my weary soul in Thee;
I give Thee back the life I owe
that in Thine ocean depths, its flow
May richer, fuller be.

GEORGE MATHESON

Christianity does not think of a man
finally submitting to the power of God;
it thinks of him as finally surrendering to
the love of God. It is not that man's will is
crushed, but that man's heart is broken.

WILLIAM BARCLAY

Abandon yourself utterly for the
love of God, **and in this way you**
will become *truly happy*.

ST. HENRY SUSO

Just as the sun shines on all the trees and flowers
as if each were the only one on earth, so does
God care for all souls in a special manner.

ST. THÉRÈSE OF LISIEUX

Incomprehensible and immutable is the love of God. For it was not after we were reconciled to Him by the blood of His Son that He began to love us, but He loved us before the foundation of the world, that with His only begotten Son we, too, might be sons of God before we were any thing at all.

AUGUSTINE

Thank You, Lord, for Your love. Your love is boundless, infinite, and eternal. Today, let me pause and reflect on Your love for me, and let me share that love with everyone who crosses my path. And, as an expression of my love for You, Lord, let me share the saving message of Your Son, Jesus, with a world in desperate need of His peace.

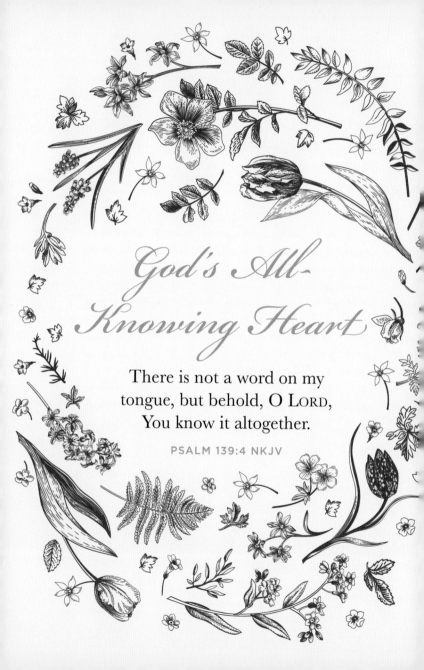

God's All-Knowing Heart

There is not a word on my tongue, but behold, O LORD, You know it altogether.

PSALM 139:4 NKJV

The heart of God is all-knowing. Even when nobody else is watching, God is watching. Even when we believe that the consequences of our actions will be known only to ourselves, our Creator sees our actions, and He responds accordingly. Ours is a God who, in His own time and in His own way, rewards righteousness and punishes sin. It's as simple as that.

Nothing that we say or do escapes the watchful eye of our Lord. God understands that we are not perfect, and He understands that we will inevitably make mistakes, but He wants us to live according to His rules, not ours. And when we go our own way, He does not protect us from the natural consequences of our mistakes.

The next time that you're tempted to say something that you shouldn't say or do something that you shouldn't do, remember that you can't keep secrets from the all-knowing heart of God. So don't even try!

God knows instantly and effortlessly all matter and all matters, all mind and every mind, all spirit and all spirits, all being and every being, all creaturehood and all creatures, every plurality and all pluralities, all law and every law, all relations, all causes, all thoughts, all mysteries, all enigmas, all feeling, all desires, every unuttered secret, all thrones and dominions, all personalities, all things visible and invisible in heaven and in earth, motion, space, time, life, death, good, evil, heaven, and hell.

A. W. TOZER

What can 'scape *the eye of God*, all-seeing, or deceive His heart, omniscient?

JOHN MILTON

Anyone can count the seeds in an apple, but only God can count the number of apples in a seed.

ROBERT SCHULLER

Before God created the universe,
He already had *you in mind.*

ERWIN LUTZER

Our heavenly Father wants nothing but the best for any of us, and only He knows what that is, for He is All-wise, the Omniscient.

ELISABETH ELLIOT

Dear Lord, You are the source of all wisdom, and You are my Teacher. I will study Your Word, and I will seek Your will. Today, I will stand upon the truth that You reveal, and I will share Your wisdom with my family, with my friends, and with the world. Amen.

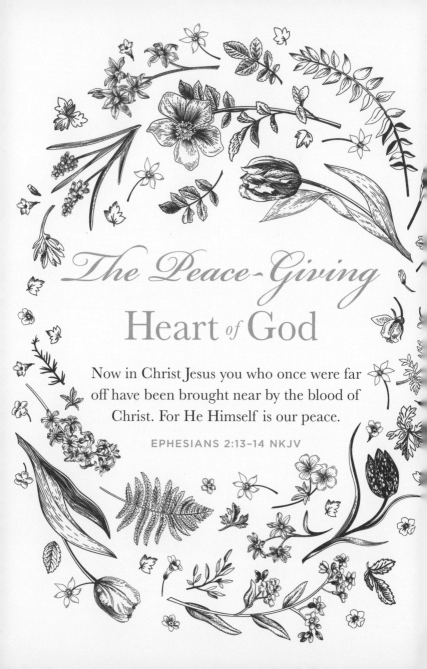

The Peace-Giving
Heart of God

Now in Christ Jesus you who once were far off have been brought near by the blood of Christ. For He Himself is our peace.

EPHESIANS 2:13–14 NKJV

The beautiful words of John 14:27 remind us that the heart of God is the source of our peace: "Peace I leave with you, My peace I give to you; not as the world gives do I give to you. Let not your heart be troubled, neither let it be afraid." Jesus offers us peace, not as the world gives, but as He alone gives. We, as believers, can accept His peace or ignore it.

When we accept the peace of Jesus Christ into our hearts, our lives are transformed. And then, because we possess the gift of peace, we can share that gift with fellow Christians, family members, friends, and associates. If, on the other hand, we choose to ignore the gift of peace—for whatever reason—we cannot share what we do not possess.

Today, as a gift to yourself, to your family, and to your friends, claim the inner peace that is your spiritual birthright: the peace of Jesus Christ that "surpasses all understanding" (Philippians 4:7 NKJV). It is offered freely; it has been paid for in full; it is yours for the asking. So, ask. And then share.

Peace does not mean to be in a place where there is no noise, trouble, or hard work. Peace means to be in the midst of all those things and still be calm in your heart.

CATHERINE MARSHALL

I believe that in every time and place it is within our power to acquiesce in the will of God—and *what peace it brings* to do so!

ELISABETH ELLIOT

It is what Jesus is, not what we are, that gives rest to the soul. If we would at once overcome Satan and have peace with God, it must be by "looking unto Jesus." . . . Let His death, His sufferings . . . His glories, His intercession be fresh upon thy mind.

C. H. SPURGEON

A great many people are trying to make peace,
but that has already been done. God has not left
it for us to do; all we have to do is to enter into it.

D. L. MOODY

**The better you become acquainted
with God, the *less tensions* you feel
and the *more peace* you possess.**

CHARLES L. ALLEN

*The world talks about peace, but only You, Lord,
can give a perfect and lasting peace. True peace
comes through the Prince of Peace, and His peace
passes all understanding. Help me to accept His
peace—and share it—this day and forever. Amen.*

The Purpose-Filled
Heart *of* God

We know that all things work together
for good to those who love God,
to those who are the called
according to His purpose.

ROMANS 8:28 NKJV

God has a plan for your life—a plan that is near and dear to His heart. If you genuinely seek to fulfill God's plan for your life, then you must make decisions that are pleasing to Him. The most important decision of your life is, of course, your commitment to accept God's Son as your personal Lord and Savior. And, once your eternal destiny is secured, you will undoubtedly ask yourself the question "What now, Lord?" If you earnestly seek God's will, you will find it . . . in time.

Life is best lived on purpose. And purpose, like everything else in the universe, begins in the heart of God. Whether you realize it or not, God has a direction for your life, a divine calling, a path along which He intends to lead you. When you welcome God into your heart and establish a genuine relationship with Him, He will begin—and He will continue—to make His purposes known.

Sometimes, God's intentions will be clear to you; other times, God's plan will seem uncertain at best. But even on those difficult days when you are unsure which way to turn, you must never lose sight of these overriding facts: God created you for a reason, He has important work for you to do, and He's waiting patiently for you to do it. So why not begin today?

God possesses infinite knowledge and awareness which is uniquely His. At all times, even in the midst of any type of suffering, I can realize that He knows, loves, watches, understands, and more than that, He has a purpose.

BILLY GRAHAM

If God's purpose for your job is that you serve the human community, then the way to *serve God best* is to do the job as well as it can be done.

TIMOTHY KELLER

When the dream in our heart is one that God has planted there, a strange happiness flows into us. At that moment, all of the spiritual resources of the universe are released to help us. Our praying is then at one with the will of God and becomes a channel for the Creator's purposes for us and our world.

CATHERINE MARSHALL

Nothing that comes to me is void of *divine purpose*. **In seeking to see the whole with God's eyes, we can** *find the peace* **which human events so often destroy.**

ELISABETH ELLIOT

God has His reasons. He has His purposes. Ours is an intentional God, brimming over with motive and mission. He never does things capriciously or decides with the flip of a coin.

JONI EARECKSON TADA

Dear Lord, let Your purposes be my purposes. Let Your priorities be my priorities. Let Your will be my will. Let Your Word be my guide. And let me grow in faith and in wisdom today and every day. Amen.

Nothing that comes to me
is void of *divine purpose*.
In seeking to see the whole
with God's eyes, we can find
the peace which human
events so often destroy.

ELISABETH ELLIOT

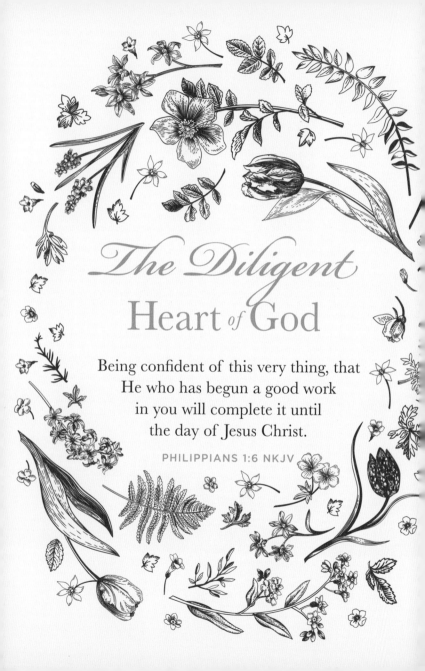

The Diligent
Heart *of* God

Being confident of this very thing, that
He who has begun a good work
in you will complete it until
the day of Jesus Christ.

PHILIPPIANS 1:6 NKJV

When many of us look back on our lives, we can see half-completed projects, relationships that had potential but didn't quite get off the ground, good intentions that were never acted upon—but God is not like that. He has never started something that He hasn't finished. His workmanship is the product of a diligent heart—a heart committed to finishing what He begins.

The diligent heart of God is clearly demonstrated in many ways; His commitment is revealed to each of us through the gift of His Son. Romans 5:8 tells us, "But God demonstrates His own love toward us, in that while we were still sinners, Christ died for us" (NKJV). Having paid that tremendous price for us, you can be sure that God will not give up on you until His good work is completed on the day of Jesus Christ.

Are you worried that God will give up on you? Have you thought that maybe He has washed His hands of you in disgust? Then put those fears to rest. Through thick and thin, God will hang in there with you until the great work He began in you on the day that you accepted Christ as your Savior is finished. His diligent heart will not allow Him to do anything less.

The Bible also tells us that our obedience to Christ and our love for fellow Christians are evidences of true, saving faith. The capstone resting on the pillars is the inner assurance that the Holy Spirit gives to us. The Spirit points to the truths of God's Word, the sufficiency of Christ's work, the reality of our faith, and the evidences of our obedience and love.

KURT DEHAAN

If you aim at and seek after nothing but the *pleasure of God* **and the welfare of your neighbor, you will enjoy** *freedom within*.

THOMAS À KEMPIS

We ought then, beloved brothers, to remember and to know, that when we call God Father, we ought to act as God's children. Then, He can take as much pleasure in considering us His sons as we do in thinking of Him as our Father.

ST. CYPRIAN OF CARTHAGE

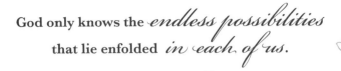

God only knows the *endless possibilities* **that lie enfolded** *in each of us*.

LILIAS TROTTER

Any patch of sunlight in a wood will show you something about the sun which you could never get from reading books on astronomy. These pure and spontaneous pleasures are "patches of Godlight" in the woods of our experience.

C. S. LEWIS

Dear Lord, I thank You that You never leave anything undone. I rejoice that on the day of the Lord Jesus I will be made complete and whole. Until that day, I thank You that You are at work in my life through Your Holy Spirit and that He will guide and direct me as You transform me into the image of Your Son, Jesus. Amen.

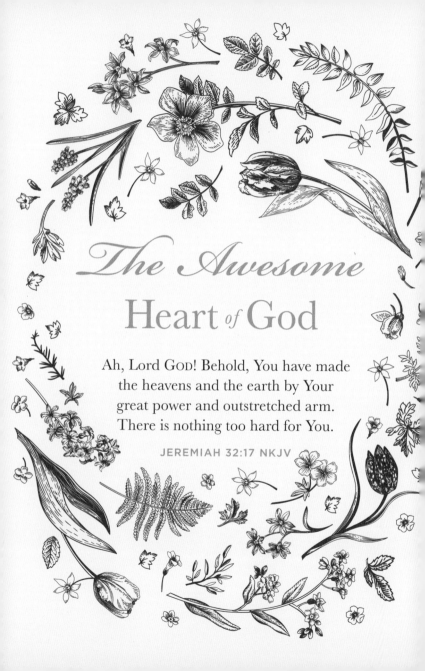

The Awesome
Heart *of* God

Ah, Lord GOD! Behold, You have made
the heavens and the earth by Your
great power and outstretched arm.
There is nothing too hard for You.

JEREMIAH 32:17 NKJV

The expression *awesome* has become a catchphrase in our society. We say that this is awesome and that is awesome, but in reality, there is only one thing that truly can claim that title—God. Nowhere is God's awesomeness reflected more intimately than in the awesome love that flows from His heart to ours. God's ability to love is not burdened by boundaries or by limitations. The love that flows from His awesome heart is infinite and beyond our comprehension.

And while we cannot fully *understand* the awesome heart of God, we *can* praise it, worship it, and marvel at its beauty.

When we worship God with faith and assurance and place Him at the absolute center of our lives, we invite His love into our hearts. In turn, we grow to love Him more deeply as we sense His love for us. Augustine wrote, "I love You, Lord, not doubtingly, but with absolute certainty. Your Word beat upon my heart until I fell in love with You, and now the universe and everything in it tells me to love You."

Let us pray that we, too, will turn our hearts to the Creator, knowing with certainty that His awesome heart has ample room for each of us, and that we, in turn, must make room in our hearts for Him.

He upholds the whole creation, founded the earth,
and still sustains it by the word of His power.
What cannot He do in the affairs of families
and kingdoms, far beyond our conception and
expectation, who hangs the earth upon nothing?

MATTHEW HENRY

**Our God is an *awesome God*.
There is *thunder* in His footsteps
and *lightning* in His fists.**

RICH MULLINS

Our evangelical culture tends to take the awesome
reality of a transcendent God who is worthy
to be feared and downsize Him so He could fit
into our "buddy system." The way we talk about
Him, the way we pray, and, more strikingly, the
way we live shows that we have somehow lost
our sense of being appropriately awestruck in
the presence of a holy and all-powerful God.

JOSEPH STOWELL

An awe for *the composer, God,*
is necessary before a pastor can fully
understand *his score, the Bible.*

FRED SMITH

*Dear Lord, for the love You have shown me and
the blessings You have given me, I stand in awe
of You. I thank You, and I praise You. Your Son
died so that I might receive the blessing of eternal
love and eternal life. May I remain awestruck
today, tomorrow, and forever, Lord, for Your love,
for Your mercy, and for Your Son. Amen.*

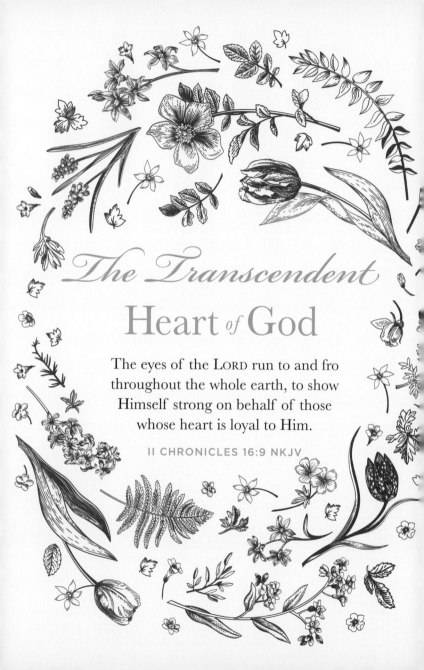

The Transcendent
Heart of God

The eyes of the LORD run to and fro
throughout the whole earth, to show
Himself strong on behalf of those
whose heart is loyal to Him.

II CHRONICLES 16:9 NKJV

Have you ever thought about how God's heart transcends time and space? It reaches beyond the stars, and it reaches into the darkest, smallest corner of every human being.

God sees *everything* (Job 28:24). And when God sees you reach out to Him, He responds (Psalm 145:18)—no "ifs, ands, or buts"—and no waiting in line for a ticket.

The words of Romans 8 make this promise: "For I am persuaded that neither death nor life, nor angels nor principalities nor powers, nor things present nor things to come, nor height nor depth, nor any other created thing, shall be able to separate us from the love of God which is in Christ Jesus our Lord" (vv. 38–39 NKJV). There is no time or place where God's heart is not available to you.

Take God at His word and welcome His Son into your heart. When you do, God's transcendent love will surround you and transform you, now and forever.

God is in all things and in all places. There is no place or thing in this world in which God is not truly present. Just as wherever birds fly they always encounter the air, so also wherever we go or wherever we are we find God present.

ST. FRANCIS DE SALES

Begin where we will,

God is there first.

A. W. TOZER

A heathen philosopher once asked, "Where is God?" The Christian answered, "Let me first ask you, where is He not?"

JOHN ARROWSMITH

A sense of deity is inscribed

on every heart.

JOHN CALVIN

To adore is to be drawn away from my own preoccupations and into the presence of Jesus. It means letting go of what I want, desire, and have planned and fully trusting in Jesus and His love.

HENRI NOUWEN

Dear God, You are nearer to me than the air that I breathe. Help me to feel Your presence in every situation and in every circumstance. You are with me, Lord, in times of celebration and in times of sorrow. You are with me when I am strong and when I am weak. You never leave my side, even when it seems to me that You are far away. Today and every day, dear God, let me feel You and acknowledge Your presence so that others, too, might come to know You through me. Amen.

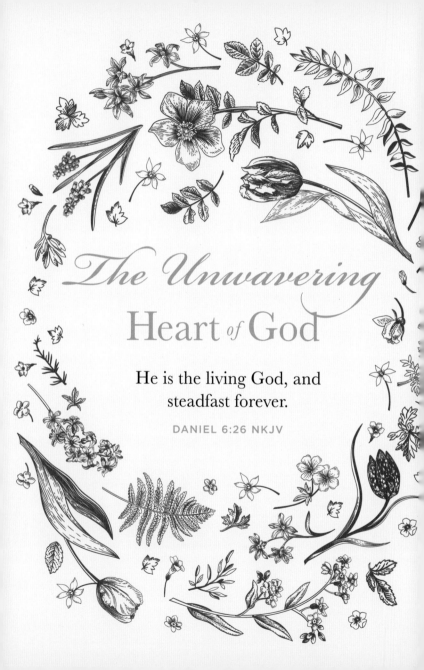

The Unwavering
Heart of God

He is the living God, and
steadfast forever.

DANIEL 6:26 NKJV

God is steadfast in His willingness to protect us. We, in turn, must be steadfast in our willingness to be protected! In other words, we must willingly accept the protection that flows freely from the unwavering heart of God. This point is illustrated by the familiar story found in Mark 4:35–41: When a terrible storm rose quickly on the Sea of Galilee, the disciples were afraid. Although they had witnessed many miracles, the disciples feared for their lives, so they turned to Jesus, and He calmed the waters and the wind.

Sometimes, we, like the disciples, feel threatened by the storms of life. When we are fearful, we, too, can turn to Christ for comfort and for courage. In life's darkest moments, we can depend upon the unwavering love of our perfect heavenly Father.

The next time you find yourself facing a fear-provoking situation, remember that the One who calmed the wind and the waves is also your personal Savior. Then ask yourself which is stronger—your faith or your fear. The answer should be obvious: Whatever your challenge, God can handle it. Your job is to let Him.

God is the great reality. His resources are available and endless. His promises are real and glorious, beyond our wildest dreams.

J. B. PHILLIPS

The stars may fall, but God's promises will stand and be fulfilled.

J. I. PACKER

We must depend upon the performance of the promise when all the ways leading up to it are shut up.

MATTHEW HENRY

The Lord may not come when you want Him, but He's always going to *be there on time*.

LOUIS GOSSETT JR.

God does not give us everything we want, but He does *fulfill His promises*, **leading us along the best and straightest paths to Himself.**

DIETRICH BONHOEFFER

Heavenly Father, sometimes I am troubled, and sometimes I grow weary. When I am weak, Lord, give me strength. When I am discouraged, renew me. When I am fearful, let me feel Your healing touch. Let me always trust in Your steadfastness, Lord, and let me draw strength from knowing that You are always there for me. Amen.

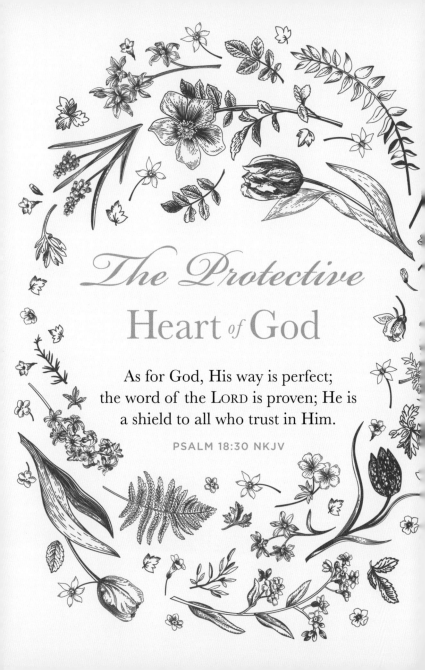

The Protective
Heart of God

As for God, His way is perfect;
the word of the LORD is proven; He is
a shield to all who trust in Him.

PSALM 18:30 NKJV

Because we are imperfect human beings living imperfect lives, we worry. Even though we, as Christians, have the assurance of salvation—even though we, as believers, have the promise of God's love and protection—we find ourselves fretting over the countless details of everyday life. Jesus understood our concerns, and He addressed them.

In Matthew 6, Jesus makes it clear that the heart of God is a protective, caring heart:

Therefore I say to you, do not worry about your life, what you will eat or what you will drink; nor about your body, what you will put on. Is not life more than food and the body more than clothing? Look at the birds of the air, for they neither sow nor reap nor gather into barns; yet your heavenly Father feeds them. Are you not of more value than they? Which of you by worrying can add one cubit to his stature? . . . Therefore do not worry about tomorrow, for tomorrow will worry about its own things. Sufficient for the day is its own trouble (vv. 25–27, 34 NKJV).

Maybe you are uncertain about your future, your finances, your relationships, or your health. Or perhaps you are simply a worrier by nature. If so, make Matthew 6 a regular part of your daily Bible reading. This beautiful passage will remind you that God still sits in His heaven and you are His beloved child. Then, perhaps, you will worry a little less and trust God a little more, and that's as it should be because God is trustworthy—and you are protected.

**A God *wise enough* to create me
and the world I live in is wise enough
to *watch out for me*.**

PHILIP YANCEY

If God has you in the palm of His hand and your real
life is secure in Him, then you can venture forth—
into the places and relationships, the challenges, the
very heart of the storm—and you will be safe there.

PAULA RINEHART

**Worry is not believing God
will get it right.**

TIMOTHY KELLER

Happy and strong and brave shall we be—
able to endure all things, and to do all things—
if we believe that every day, every hour, every
moment of our life is in God's hands.

HENRY VAN DYKE

Who is it that is your Shepherd? The Lord! Oh, my friends, what a wonderful announcement! The Lord God of heaven and earth, and Almighty Creator of all things, He who holds the universe in His hand as though it were a very little thing. He is your shepherd and has charged Himself with the care and keeping of you, as a shepherd is charged with the care and keeping of his sheep. If your hearts could really take in this thought, you would never have a fear or a care again; for with such a Shepherd how could it be possible for you ever to want for any good thing?

HANNAH WHITALL SMITH

Thank You, dear Lord, for Your protection. In a dangerous world, I rejoice to know that Your heart is concerned with my protection. For that I give You the praise and the glory. Forgive me for worrying about things that You are already taking care of. Help me to trust You instead of worrying, for I know You are my Protector and Provider. Amen.

When terrible things happen . . .
there are two choices, and only two:
We can trust God or we can defy Him.
We believe that God is God, He's still
got the whole world in His hands and
knows exactly what He's doing, or we
must believe that He is not God and
we are at the awful mercy
of mere chance.

ELISABETH ELLIOT

The Sovereign
Heart *of* God

Let the heavens rejoice, and let the earth be glad; and let them say among the nations, "The Lᴏʀᴅ reigns."

I CHRONICLES 16:31 NKJV

The heart of God is sovereign; it reigns over all God's creation, including you. Your challenge is to recognize God's sovereignty and live in accordance with His commandments. Sometimes, of course, this is easier said than done.

Proverbs 3:6 gives you guidance: "In all your ways acknowledge Him, and He shall direct your paths" (NKJV). When you think about it, the words in this verse make a powerful promise: If you acknowledge God's sovereignty over every aspect of your life, He will guide your path. That's an important promise.

So, as you prayerfully consider the path that God intends for you to take, here are some things you should do: You should study His Word and be ever-watchful for His signs. You should associate with fellow believers who will encourage your spiritual growth. You should listen carefully to that inner voice that speaks to you in the quiet moments of your daily devotionals. And, as you continually seek God's unfolding purpose for your life, you should be patient.

Your heavenly Father may not always reveal Himself as quickly as you would like. But rest assured: God is sovereign. At the right time, in the right way, His sovereign heart will bring to pass what is right and good.

Knowing God's sovereignty and
unconditional love **imparts a**
beauty to life **. . . and to you.**

KAY ARTHUR

Jesus did not promise to change the circumstances
around us. He promised great peace and
pure joy to those who would learn to believe
that God actually controls all things.

CORRIE TEN BOOM

Waiting is the hardest kind of work,
but *God knows best,* **and we may**
joyfully leave all in His hands.

LOTTIE MOON

God's sovereignty is the attribute by which He rules
His entire creation, and to be sovereign, God must
be all-knowing, all-powerful, and absolutely free.

A. W. TOZER

When terrible things happen . . . there are
two choices, and only two: We can trust God
or we can defy Him. We believe that God
is God, He's still got the whole world in His
hands and knows exactly what He's doing, or
we must believe that He is not God and we
are at the awful mercy of mere chance.

ELISABETH ELLIOT

*Lord, when my path is steep and my heart is troubled,
let me trust in You. When I become discouraged or
anxious, let me depend upon You. When I lose faith in
this world, let me never lose faith in You. Remind me,
Lord, that in every situation and in every season of
life, You will love me and protect me. And, with You
as my Protector, Lord, I need never lose hope because
You remain sovereign today and forever. Amen.*

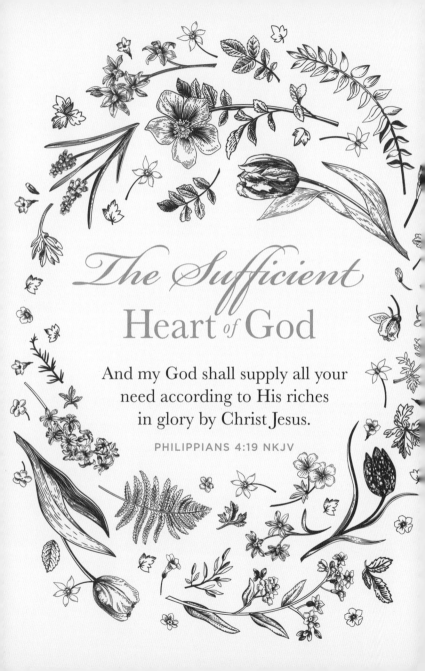

The Sufficient
Heart *of* God

And my God shall supply all your
need according to His riches
in glory by Christ Jesus.

PHILIPPIANS 4:19 NKJV

O f this you can be sure: The heart of God is sufficient to meet your needs. No matter what dangers you may face or heartbreaks you might endure, God is with you. And He stands ready to provide for whatever you truly need.

The psalmist writes, "Weeping may endure for a night, but joy comes in the morning" (Psalm 30:5 NKJV). But when we are suffering, the morning may seem very far away. It is not. God promises that He is "near to those who have a broken heart" (Psalm 34:18 NKJV). In times of intense sadness, we must turn to Him, and we must encourage our friends and family members to find their sufficiency in Him as well.

If you are experiencing the intense pain of a recent loss, or if you are still mourning a loss from long ago, perhaps you are now ready to begin the next stage of your journey with God. If so, be mindful of this fact: The loving heart of God is sufficient to meet any challenge, including yours. Trust the sufficient heart of God.

I grew up learning to be self-reliant, but now, to grow up in Christ, I must unlearn self-reliance and learn self-distrust in light of His all-sufficiency.

MARY MORRISON SUGGS

He who has God and many
other things has no more than
he who has God alone.

C. S. LEWIS

The last and greatest lesson that the soul has to learn is the fact that God, and God alone, is enough for all its needs. This is the lesson that all His dealings with us are meant to teach; and this is the crowning discovery of our whole Christian life. God is enough!

HANNAH WHITALL SMITH

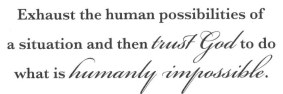

Exhaust the human possibilities of a situation and then *trust God* **to do what is** *humanly impossible*.

LILIAS TROTTER

Jesus has been consistently affectionate and true to us. He has shared His great wealth with us. How can we doubt the all-powerful, all-sufficient Lord?

C. H. SPURGEON

You have promised, Lord, that You will not give me any more than I can bear. You have promised to lift me out of my grief and despair. Remind me that Your grace is sufficient for me. You have promised to put a new song on my lips. I thank You, Lord, for Your sufficiency. Restore me, heal me, and use me as You will. Amen.

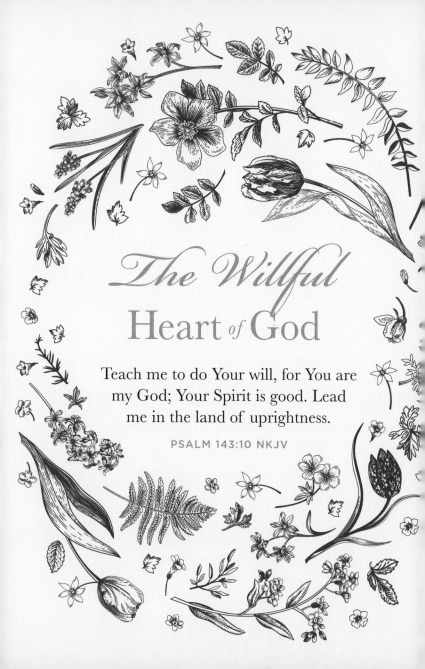

The Willful

Heart of God

Teach me to do Your will, for You are
my God; Your Spirit is good. Lead
me in the land of uprightness.

PSALM 143:10 NKJV

God has a plan for our world and for our lives. God does not do things by accident; He is willful and intentional. Unfortunately for us, we simply cannot always understand the willful heart of God. Why? Because we are mortal beings with limited understanding. Thus, we can never fully comprehend the will of God. But as believers in a benevolent heavenly Father, we must always trust the will of God.

Before His crucifixion, Jesus went to the Mount of Olives and poured out His heart to God (Luke 22). Jesus knew of the agony that He was destined to endure, but He also knew that God's will must be done. We, like our Savior, face trials that bring fear and trembling to the very depths of our souls. But like Christ, we, too, must ultimately seek God's will, not our own.

As this day unfolds, seek God's will and obey His Word. When you entrust your life to Him completely and without reservation, He will give you the strength to meet any challenge, the courage to face any trial, and the wisdom to live in His righteousness and in His peace.

Doing God's will is never hard. The only thing that is hard is not doing His will.

OSWALD CHAMBERS

True faith does not so much attempt to manipulate God to do our will as it does to position us *to do His will.*

PHILIP YANCEY

Yielding to the will of God is simply letting His Holy Spirit have His way in our lives. Continual prayer allows us to be "filled with the Spirit," as God commands us.

SHIRLEY DOBSON

No one may prefer his own will to the will of God, but in everything we must seek and *do the will of God.*

ST. BASIL THE GREAT

God alone is in control of circumstances. You are safer in a famine *in His will* than in a palace *out of His will*.

WARREN WIERSBE

Dear Lord, You are the Creator of the universe, and I know that Your plan for my life is grander than I can imagine. Let Your purposes be my purposes. Let Your will be my will. When I am confused, give me clarity. When I am worried, give me strength. Let me be Your faithful servant, Lord, always seeking Your guidance and Your will for my life. Let me live this day and every day according to Your commandments and with the assurance of Your promises, in Jesus' name I pray. Amen.

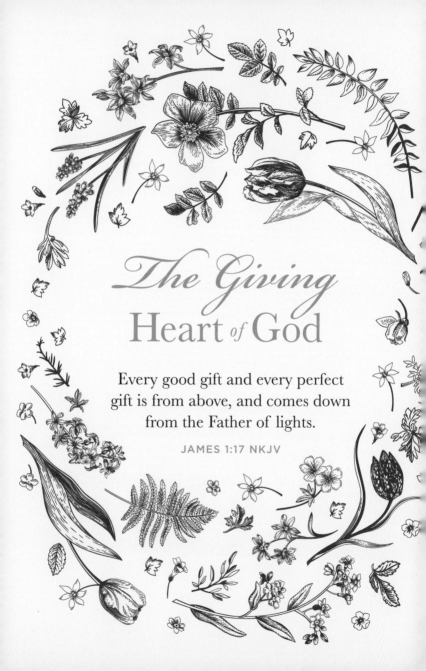

The Giving
Heart of God

Every good gift and every perfect
gift is from above, and comes down
from the Father of lights.

JAMES 1:17 NKJV

The heart of God overflows with gifts for His children, and you are no exception. God has given you a special array of talents and opportunities, and you should be thankful. But you should also beware: Neither natural talent nor social position will guarantee your success. Your gifts from God must be cultivated and nurtured; otherwise, they will go unused, and God's gift to you will be squandered.

The gifts that you possess are precious treasures from the Giver of all things good. Do you have a spiritual gift? Share it. Do you have a testimony about the things that Christ has done for you? Don't leave your story untold. Do you possess financial resources? Share them. Do you have particular talents? Hone your skills and use them for God's glory.

When you hoard (or squander) the blessings that God has given you, you are living in rebellion against His commandments. But, when you obey God by sharing His gifts freely and without fanfare, you invite Him to bless you more and more.

Today, be a faithful steward of your talents and treasures. And then prepare yourself for even *greater* blessings that are sure to come.

We must stir up *the gift of God.*
Like sugar in the lemonade, it may be
there, but it needs to be set in motion.

VANCE HAVNER

God is the giver, and we are the receivers. And
His richest gifts are bestowed not upon those
who do the greatest things, but upon those
who accept His abundance and His grace.

HANNAH WHITALL SMITH

God gives His gifts where He finds
the vessel empty enough to receive them.

C. S. LEWIS

The Lord has abundantly blessed me all
of my life. I'm not trying to pay Him back
for all of His wonderful gifts; I just realize
that He gave them to me to give away.

LISA WHELCHEL

One thing taught large in the Holy Scriptures is that while God gives His gifts freely, He will require a strict accounting of them at the end of the road. Each man is personally responsible for his store, be it large or small, and will be required to explain his use of it before the judgment seat of Christ.

A. W. TOZER

Lord, You loved me before I was even born; You sent Your Son, Jesus, to redeem me from my sins; You have given me the gift of eternal life. I will be thankful always, and I will praise You always. Today, I will share the priceless gifts that I have received: I will share my joy, my possessions, and my faith with others. And I will be a humble giver, Lord, so that all the glory might be Yours. Amen.

The Helping
Heart of God

I will lift up my eyes to the hills—
from whence comes my help?
My help comes from the LORD,
who made heaven and earth.

PSALM 121:1–2 NKJV

The heart of God yearns to help His children. But sometimes they resist His help by disobeying His commandments. Never allow yourself to fall into that spiritual trap. God's commandments were not given to make life miserable for you. Indeed, just the opposite. They were given to help you avoid many of the pitfalls of life.

God's helping heart yearns to keep His children safe. He longs to help them live full and satisfying lives. Jesus said, "I have come that they may have life, and that they may have it more abundantly" (John 10:10 NKJV).

Do you want to live an abundant life? Then let God's helping heart show you the way. Study His Word and apply it to your daily life. God's helping heart is as near as your Bible.

God provides for those who trust.

GEORGE HERBERT

Fear not, I am with you, O be not dismayed,
for I am your God and will still give you aid; I'll
strengthen you, help you, and cause you to stand,
upheld by My righteous, omnipotent hand.

GEORGE KEITH AND ROBERT KEEN

O God, *our help* in ages past,
our hope for years to come,
Our shelter from the stormy
blast, and our *eternal home*!

ISAAC WATTS

The Shepherd will not always replenish you in
the same way; His response to you will always
perfectly correspond to your present need.

HENRY BLACKABY

When you live a surrendered life,

God is willing and able to

provide for your every need.

CORRIE TEN BOOM

Lord, You have promised never to leave me or forsake me. You are always with me, helping me and encouraging me. Whatever this day may bring, I thank You for Your love and for Your strength. Let me lean upon You, Father, this day and forever. Amen.

Your heavenly Father
loves you in ways that you
cannot fully understand.
God's heart is filled with
care, concern, compassion,
empathy, and love.

ELISABETH ELLIOT

The Saving
Heart *of* God

For God so loved the world that
He gave His only begotten Son, that
whoever believes in Him should not
perish but have everlasting life.

JOHN 3:16 NKJV

The heart of God is a saving heart. The familiar words of John 3:16 remind us of a profound truth: God loves each of us so much that He sent His Son to die for our sins.

Your heavenly Father offers you the priceless gift of eternal life. How will you respond? Christ sacrificed His life on the cross so that you might be with Him throughout eternity. This gift, freely given from God's only begotten Son, is a priceless possession, a treasure beyond price, yet it is freely offered to you.

God is waiting patiently for each of us to accept the gift of eternal life. Let us claim Christ's gift today. Let us walk with the Savior, let us love Him, let us praise Him, and let us share His message of salvation with the world.

The more you understand how your
salvation **isn't about your behavior, the**
more radically your *behavior* **will change.**

TIMOTHY KELLER

God is glorified when people believe His gospel,
love His Son, and accept His diagnosis of
their greatest need, which is forgiveness of sin.
You certainly benefit from God's provision of
salvation, but you exist for the glory of God.

JOHN MACARTHUR

The *grace* **that saves them is the free**
undeserved *goodness* **and** *favor* **of God.**

MATTHEW HENRY

Before a man can be saved, he must feel a
consuming spiritual hunger. Where a hungry heart
is found, we may be sure that God was there first.

A. W. TOZER

God proved His love on the cross. When Christ hung, and bled, and died, it was God saying to the world, *"I love you."*

My salvation is in You, O Lord. My soul finds rest in You through Your Son, Jesus Christ. The gift of salvation brings meaning to my life on earth because I possess the assurance of eternal life with You in heaven. I will praise You and honor You, Father, today and forever. Amen.

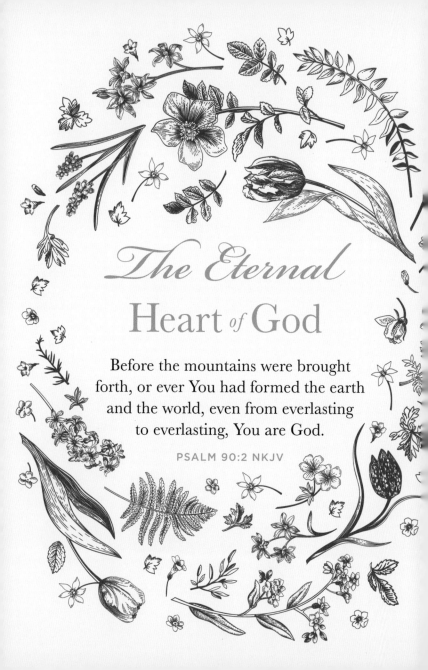

The Eternal
Heart *of* God

Before the mountains were brought
forth, or ever You had formed the earth
and the world, even from everlasting
to everlasting, You are God.

PSALM 90:2 NKJV

The heart of God is eternal and unchanging. Before God laid the foundations of our universe, He was a being of infinite power and love, and He will remain so throughout all eternity.

We humans are in a state of constant change. We are born, we grow, we mature, and we die. Along the way, we experience the inevitable joys and hardships of life. And we face the inevitable changes that are the result of our own mortality.

But God never changes. His love never ceases, His wisdom never fails, and His promises endure, unbroken, forever. He "is the same yesterday, today, and forever" (Hebrews 13:8 NKJV).

Place your trust in an eternal, unchanging God. Rest assured that His eternal heart will love you as much tomorrow as He does today and forever.

Rejoice, that the *immortal God is born,*
so that mortal man may *live in eternity.*

JAN HUS

[God] is not affected by our mutability; our changes
do not alter Him. When we are restless, He remains
serene and calm; when we are low, selfish, mean,
or dispirited, He is still the unalterable I Am, the
same yesterday, today, and forever, in whom is no
variableness, neither shadow of turning. What God
is in Himself, not what we may chance to feel Him
in this or that moment to be, that is our hope.

FREDERICK WILLIAM ROBERTSON

In God there is no *was* or *will be,*
but a continuous and unbroken *is.*
In Him history and prophecy are
one and the same.

A. W. TOZER

Christ is like . . . a river [that] is continually flowing. There are always fresh supplies of water coming from the fountain-head continually, so that a man may live by it, and be supplied with water all his life. So Christ is an ever-flowing fountain; He is continually supplying His people, and the fountain is not spent. They who live upon Christ, may have fresh supplies from Him to all eternity; they may have an increase of blessedness that is new, and new still, and which never will come to an end.

JONATHAN EDWARDS

Dear Lord, I praise You that You are eternal. There was never a time when You did not exist, nor will there be a time when You will not be. Thank You that You will never change and that You will never stop loving me. You alone are the solid rock on which I build my life, and You will never be shaken. I am so grateful that in this changing world, You are constant and dependable, Lord. Amen.

The Attentive
Heart *of* God

I know the thoughts that I think toward you, says the LORD, thoughts of peace and not of evil, to give you a future and a hope. Then you will call upon Me and go and pray to Me, and I will listen to you.

JEREMIAH 29:11–12 NKJV

God is not distant, and He is not disinterested either. To the contrary, your heavenly Father is very interested in everything about you. In fact, God knows precisely what you need and when you need it. But, He still wants to talk with you, and if you're a faithful believer, you should want to talk to Him too.

Jesus made it clear to His disciples that even though God knew their needs, they should pray always—and so should we. Genuine, heartfelt prayer changes things, and it changes us too. When we lift our hearts to our Father in heaven, we open ourselves to a never-ending source of divine wisdom and infinite love.

Do you have questions that you simply can't answer? Ask for the guidance of your Creator. Do you sincerely seek the gift of everlasting love and eternal life? Accept the grace of God's only begotten Son. Whatever your need, no matter how great or small, pray about it. Instead of waiting for mealtimes or bedtimes, follow the instruction of your Savior: pray always and never lose heart. And remember: God is not simply near; He is attentive to what is happening to you, and He wants to talk with you. Now!

Even more than we *long to be heard,* **[God]** *desires to listen.*

ANGELA THOMAS

Prayer is request. The essence of request, as distinct from compulsion, is that it may or may not be granted. And if an infinitely wise Being listens to the requests of finite and foolish creatures, of course He will sometimes grant and sometimes refuse them.

C. S. LEWIS

You can talk to God because God listens. Your voice matters in heaven. He takes you very seriously. . . . Even if you stammer or stumble, even if what you have to say impresses no one, it impresses God—and He listens.

MAX LUCADO

The key to a *blessed life* **is to have a** *listening heart* **that longs to know what the** *Lord is saying.*

JIM CYMBALA

[When we pray,] the first thing we should do is to see to it that we really get an audience with God, that we really get into His very presence. Before a word of petition is offered, we should have the definite and vivid consciousness that we are talking to God, and we should believe that He is listening.

R. A. TORREY

Dear Lord, Your Holy Word commands me to pray without ceasing. And You are always listening. Let me take everything to You in prayer. When I am discouraged, let me pray. When I am lonely, let me take my sorrows to You. When I grieve, let me take my tears to You in prayer. And when I am joyful, let me offer up prayers of thanksgiving. In all things great and small, at all times, whether happy or sad, let me seek Your wisdom and Your grace, for You are continually attentive to me. Amen.

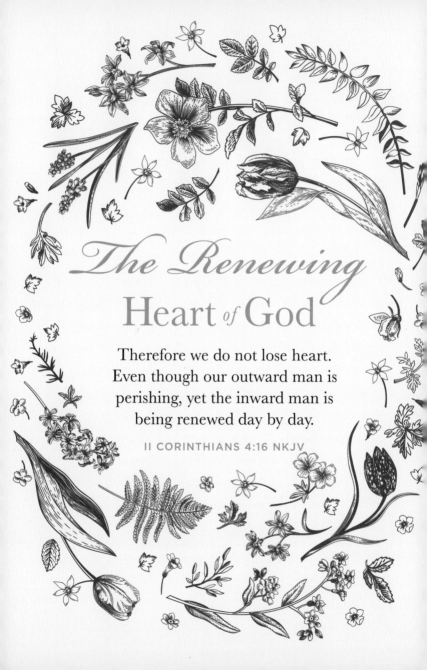

The Renewing
Heart *of* God

Therefore we do not lose heart.
Even though our outward man is
perishing, yet the inward man is
being renewed day by day.

II CORINTHIANS 4:16 NKJV

God intends that His children lead joyous lives filled with abundance and peace. But sometimes abundance and peace seem very far away. It is then that we must turn to God for renewal, and when we do, He will restore us. He promises that as we wait on Him, He will "renew [our] strength" (Isaiah 40:31 NKJV).

Are you tired or troubled? Turn your prayers toward the renewing heart of God. Are you weak or worried? Study God's Word and contemplate its meaning for your life. Are you spiritually depleted? Call upon fellow Christians to lift you up, and call upon Christ to renew your faith and your strength. When you do, you'll discover that your heavenly Father is, indeed, a God of renewal. And you will discover that He is always willing to create a new sense of wonderment and joy *in you*.

Like a spring of pure water, *God's peace in our hearts* brings cleansing and refreshment to our minds and bodies.

BILLY GRAHAM

The same voice that brought Lazarus out of the tomb raised us to newness of life.

C. H. SPURGEON

Walking with God leads to receiving His intimate counsel, and counseling leads to *deep restoration*.

JOHN ELDREDGE

The amazing thing about Jesus is that He doesn't just patch up our lives. . . . He gives us a brand-new sheet, a clean slate to start over with.

GLORIA GAITHER

No matter how badly we have failed, we can always get up and begin again. Our God is the God of *new beginnings.*

Dear Lord, You can make all things new. I am a new creature in Christ Jesus, and when I fall short in my commitment, You can renew my effort and my enthusiasm. When I am weak or worried, restore my strength; when I feel like giving up, renew my resolve—for my own sake and for the sake of Your kingdom. Amen.

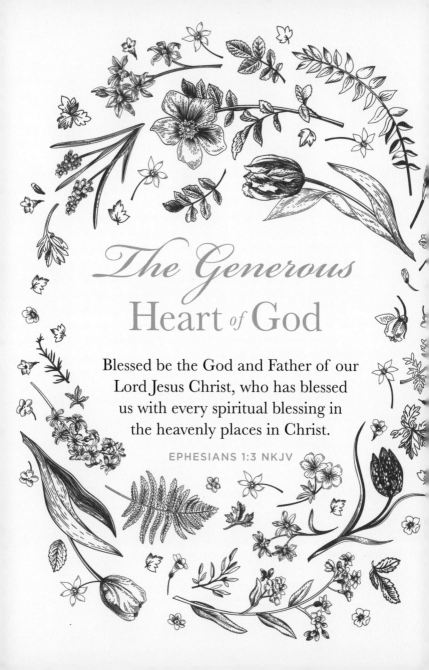

The Generous
Heart of God

Blessed be the God and Father of our
Lord Jesus Christ, who has blessed
us with every spiritual blessing in
the heavenly places in Christ.

EPHESIANS 1:3 NKJV

God's heart overflows with generosity and mercy. And as believers in a loving God, we must imitate our heavenly Father to the best of our abilities. Because God has been so incredibly generous with us, we, in turn, must be generous with others.

Jesus has much to teach us about generosity. He teaches that the most esteemed men and women are not the self-congratulatory leaders of society but are, instead, the humblest of servants (Matthew 23:11–12).

If you were being graded on generosity, how would you score? Would you earn A's in philanthropy and humility? Hopefully so. But if your grades could stand a little improvement, today is the perfect day to begin.

Today, you may feel the urge to hoard your blessings. Don't do it. Instead, give generously to your neighbors, and do so without fanfare. Find a need and fill it—humbly. Lend a helping hand and share a word of encouragement—anonymously. This is God's way.

Giving with glad and generous hearts has a way of routing out the tough old miser within us. Even the poor need to know that they can give. Just the very act of letting go of money, or some other treasure, does something within us. It destroys the demon greed.

RICHARD J. FOSTER

In Jesus, **the service of God and the service of the least of the brethren were one.**

DIETRICH BONHOEFFER

All the blessings we enjoy are divine deposits, committed to our trust on this condition, that they should be dispensed for the benefit of our neighbors.

JOHN CALVIN

Christianity, in its purest form, is nothing more than seeing Jesus. Christian service, in its purest form, is nothing more than imitating Him who we see. To see His Majesty and to imitate Him, that is the sum of Christianity.

MAX LUCADO

Following Jesus means living as obedient servants of His heavenly Father and ministering—even suffering— *for the sake of others.*

STANLEY GRENZ

Dear Lord, in my weak moments, I want to hoard all my blessings to enjoy by myself. But Your commandment, Lord, is that I become a humble servant sharing with those who need my encouragement, my help, and my love. Instill in me the same generous spirit that fills Your heart. Make me willing to give so that my life may bring praise and honor to You. Amen.

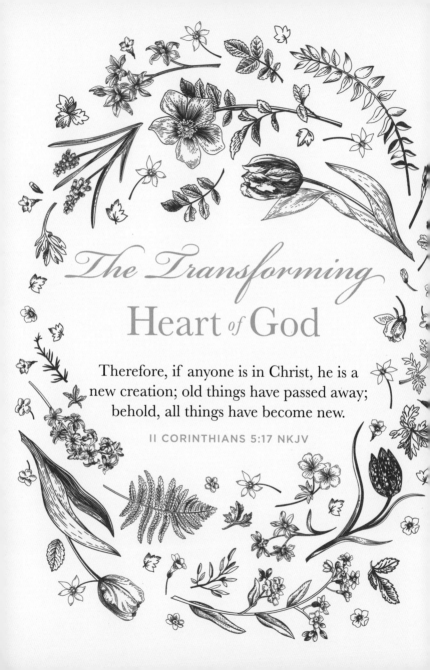

The Transforming
Heart *of* God

Therefore, if anyone is in Christ, he is a
new creation; old things have passed away;
behold, all things have become new.

II CORINTHIANS 5:17 NKJV

For many people, change is to be avoided at all costs. But the Bible makes it clear that God's ultimate goal is to change us. When we accept Christ into our hearts and genuinely invite Him to reign over our lives, we become different people—and this change is forever.

When we welcome Jesus into our hearts, an old life ends and a new life begins. God transforms our lives and gives us a completely new view of the world.

Let us, then, live out that transformed life. Each morning offers a fresh opportunity to invite Christ to rule over our hearts and our days. Each new day presents yet another opportunity to take up our cross and follow in His footsteps. Today, let us rejoice in the new life that is ours through Christ, and let us follow Him, step by step, on the transformative path He places before us.

There is no situation so chaotic that God cannot, from that situation, create something that is surpassingly good. He did it at the creation. He did it at the cross. He is doing it today.

HANDLEY MOULE

There is nothing anybody else can do that can stop God from using us. We can turn everything into *a testimony*.

CORRIE TEN BOOM

A person who really cares about his or her neighbor, a person who genuinely loves others, is a person who bears witness to the truth.

ANNE GRAHAM LOTZ

If the world controls your thinking, you are a *conformer*; if God controls your thinking, you are a *transformer*.

WARREN WIERSBE

The adventure of *new life in Christ* begins when the comfortable patterns of the old life are left behind.

DAVID ROHER

Dear Lord, thank You for making me a new creation in Christ Jesus. I confess that the life I live and the words I speak bear testimony to my transformed life. Make me a faithful servant of Your Son, Jesus, and let my testimony be worthy of You. May my words be sure and true, Lord, and let my actions point others to You. Amen.

If you genuinely trust your *heavenly Father*, and if you allow *His Son* to reign over your life, you will be held close to *God's heart*—today, tomorrow, and *forever*.

ELISABETH ELLIOT

Dear Friend,

This book was prayerfully crafted with you, the reader, in mind. Every word, every sentence, every page was thoughtfully written, designed, and packaged to encourage you—right where you are this very moment. At DaySpring, our vision is to see every person experience the life-changing message of God's love. So, as we worked through rough drafts, design changes, edits, and details, we prayed for you to deeply experience His unfailing love, indescribable peace, and pure joy. It is our sincere hope that through these Truth-filled pages your heart will be blessed, knowing that God cares about you—your desires and disappointments, your challenges and dreams.

He knows. He cares. He loves you unconditionally.

BLESSINGS!
THE DAYSPRING BOOK TEAM

Additional copies of this book and
other DaySpring titles can be purchased
at fine retailers everywhere.
Order online at <u>dayspring.com</u>
or
by phone at 1-877-751-4347